CLLAIMM
OPTIMAL RESULTS FOR INSTITUTIONAL STUDENT LEARNING

MARENA SIMMONS JONES M.Ed.

Special Touch Learning/Educational Success Publishing

The opinions expressed in this manuscript are solely the opinions of the author and do not represent the opinions or thoughts of the publisher. The author has represented and warranted full ownership and/or legal right to publish all the materials in this book.

CLLAIMM
Optimal Results For Institutional Student Learning
All Rights Reserved.
Copyright © 2015 Marena Simmons Jones M.Ed.
v2.0

Cover Photo © 2015 Marena Simmons Jones. All rights reserved - used with permission.

This book may not be reproduced, transmitted, or stored in whole or in part by any means, including graphic, electronic, or mechanical without the express written consent of the publisher except in the case of brief quotations embodied in critical articles and reviews.

Special Touch Learning/Educational Success Publishing

ISBN: 978-0-578-15777-1

PRINTED IN THE UNITED STATES OF AMERICA

CLLAIMM MODEL

There is a vital need for churches and innovative institutions to reestablish themselves as a core element to the learning process of our nation's youth. According to Marena Simmons Jones, the CLLIAMM© core values and Learning model establishes the total essential of learning at its best.

The CLLAIMM© model is a highly effective educationally diverse model that utilizes different learning modalities and learning styles such as kinesthetic, visual, auditory, and verbal in order to ensure that all students receive optimal results with their learning. Studies show that students are best reached by employing a variety of modalities in the classroom. Students exposed to a variety of learning styles have been shown to soar to optimal levels and are most able to tap into their greatest potential. Within this realm, lessons and activities are presented in innovative and exciting ways, and the results thereof help to foster confidence and success with each student.

"Growing evidence strongly suggests that a key element in meeting all our educational goals for children and youth, academic as well as social, and helping all children to reach their highest potential is social and emotional learning (SEL)" (Collaborative for Academic, Social and Emotional Learning).

CLLAIMM© – Core Values and Learning Model

1. Christian Foundation

2. Life-Skill Introduction & Financial Awareness for life

3. Leadership Empowerment

4. Academics (Education)

5. Innovative & Positive School Environment

6. Meditation

7. Motivational Speaking Sessions

CLLAIMM MODEL

1. Christian Foundation

The CLLAIMM© program model relies on building and supporting a strong Christian foundation and Godly character in all students. Academics in the CLLAIMM© model incorporate biblical principles while explicitly requiring students of all ages to learn the Word of God to build spiritual consciousness, integrity, good self-esteem, and confidence. This model builds high achievers and provides them a good foundation to make great life-decisions.

Word of God

The Bible is the framework in the CLLAIMM© program model for creating a succinct and highly effective platform of Biblical truth on which students will be able to glean a variety of life skills and grow in faith and personal awareness. With a strong Biblical foundation students are able to stand firm in Biblical truths and weather challenges that may come their way. Students are also able to apply Biblical truths to their lives and increase personal awareness and self-esteem. Students' confidence and character grows as they learn the application of the Word of God. Biblical characters and heroes of the faith are also studied, which can also serve students as Godly examples of perseverance and dedication to God.

CLLAIMM

Spiritual Conscious

Thinking about one's actions and being spiritual conscious is integral to building a strong Christian faith. Students will be exposed to methods and lessons on how to build spiritual consciousness of a Christian life. Students will be able to recognize spiritual aspects discuss with others on how their faith is forming and growing. Being a spiritually conscious Christian is important to the Body of Christ and important for children to grasp at an early age because a life built on Christ will weather the test of time. Students are able to see evidence of how God has blessed them and see how God is working in their life as they grow and become more spiritually conscious. They are also able to give testimony to others, which helps "iron sharpen iron" and "encouraging one another in the faith," as is outlined in scripture.

Integrity

Integrity in word and deed and in wanting to be the best to self and others is an aim of the CLLAIMM© model. Each student should aim to build a high level of personal and communal integrity. This model interweaves examples of integrity building as well as ways to implement skills that exhibit integrity across all areas of a student's life. Special focus and examples are provided to students, and students learn to identify and to incorporate what it means to build integrity in their lives as they grow in Christ. Integrity affects all areas of students' lives as well as has a positive effect in the school environment. A good platform of integrity is a life skill that builds a solid character.

Good self-esteem

The CLLAIMM© program model focuses on self-esteem building in all areas of students' lives. Students are infused with positive reinforcement, ways to build self-esteem, and opportunities to shine. These, coupled with a variety of learning tools, help to build confidence and in turn help a students feel good about themselves. Self-esteem is an important factor to determining success of a student. The CLLAIMM© program model seeks to build these skills early and reinforce them continually. Good self-esteem at an early age helps to create a good environment for learning. Students who feel good about what they are learning, and feel that they are capable in learning it, may have better success in the classroom. In turn, when students feels good about themselves, they feel more confident to step out and share their feelings and to explore new possibilities in learning.

2. **Life-Skill Introduction Preparedness (Part 1) & Financial Awareness (Part 2)** CLLAIMM© believes in providing students not only a well-rounded education focusing on academics, but also life-skill development for success.

CLLAIMM

The Special Touch College Preparatory model incorporates life-skill development preparedness and an aggressive hands-on and observational organized training program in order to implement a comprehensive learning model. The hands-on learning programs expose students to various extra-curricular areas such as cooking, media production, art, sports, and more. Students rotate through classes in a hands-on learning program each quarter. The Preschoolers participate in hands-on learning as part of the daily curriculum.

The objective is to expose children to the various professions, hobbies, responsibilities, and the Athletics Program. The life-skill program offers effective learning styles and allows children opportunities to express themselves and their God-given gifts and talents.

Part 1

Exposing children to various real life jobs, duties, professions, hobbies, and responsibilities helps them to have tangible and positive experiences early in their educational journeys. Students benefit from observing positive role models in life. One way to hone in on a student's interests and skills is to provide plenty of opportunities to observe a variety of jobs, hobbies, and professions in real life. Many times students limit their ideas to what they want to be in life, to what they want to accomplish in life, or to what they have seen in their families or communities. Within this model, the sky is the limit! Students are exposed to a variety of enriching options to expand their horizons and to observe careers and hobbies they may never have seen.

In addition, students are presented with a well-rounded holistic life-skills program that enables students to expand on life skills they already possess, as well as explore ones that may be new to them. Life skills are extremely important in the development of the whole child. Life skills learned at an early age open new doors of opportunity to students to enable them to soar to new heights and navigate social, economic, educational, and political systems with confidence and vigor.

Experience

The CLLAIMM© program model offers hands-on experience with a variety of life skills appropriate to age and grade level. As these skills are learned, new skills will be added to the platforms that are built. Experience is a key factor when navigating job markets and opening businesses. Students need plenty of opportunities to gain hands on experience. The life-skills program enhances a higher level of learning. These life skills are more than just activities; these skills are building blocks of success for students to use in their lives as they move forward.

Life-skills offer effective learning styles where children receive training in various subjects. The CLLAIMM©

program model presents these life skills in a wide spectrum of modalities by employing visual, kinesthetic, auditory, and verbal learning styles. Students are able to use and hone these life skills within the modalities that work best for them, as well as develop skills in areas that may need strengthening. These life skills are offered with a great deal of creativity that best encompasses the whole student, as well as offers plenty of practice for reflection, group work, and dialogue. Students are the given opportunity to share and report back their findings, and the opportunity to express their skills through art, writing, dialogue, and other media.

In addition to academics, life-skill attainment is of utmost importance. Children have God-given talents and gifts and should be afforded more opportunities to express themselves and their God-given gifts and talents. In order to discover and hone these skills and talents, they must be developed. Students often do not have a full grasp of what these talents are unless they are given the opportunities to learn new skills and develop the skills they have. Children begin to understand their gifts from exposure and doing. Many times children may not be clear on what their talents are at first, but through exposure, positive reinforcement, and guidance, students have an "aha" moment where a "light bulb" comes on. These moments are interwoven throughout the CLLAIMM © program model and allow an opportunity for educators to truly guide and

CLLAIMM MODEL

inspire students to discover, build, and develop their talents, which also helps to build other talents and skills. It is an exciting continuum to behold.

It is important to allow children, from a young age, to experience as they start to see and feel their natural gifts conform. Children, in their formative years, are able to learn skills at an amazing rate. When children are exposed to a variety of skills and are given an opportunity to hone those skills, their capabilities begin to surface. This contributes to the students' growth and sharpens their skills as they mature. This allows children to develop their interests and consider them as a part of their future.

The CLLAIMM© program model offers hands on training in a structured environment. Students are encouraged to develop and sharpen skills within a structured environment. This offers students opportunities to be guided and to develop leadership skills by leading small groups, small discussions, and hands on activities. This, exposure, expression, and development allows greater chance children's God-given gifts to become professed; it enables children to start to work within their God–given purposes as found in Jeremiah 29:11.

As children develop in these life skills, it helps them to know who they are and how they can explore their identity within their personal, academic, familial, and social realms. Moreover, as children glean Biblical truths, they are able to seek the Lord's face and will in their lives. Others come to know children as children learn to use and express their God-given gifts. This awareness helps to make navigating life easier by providing a solid academic background with life skills and opportunity to become a well-rounded person in faith. These life skills and the Biblical platform in the CLLAIMM© program model helps students make healthy and strong decisions and prepares them to set future goals in their personal lives such as college, trade school, entrepreneurship ventures, or business ownership.

Part 2

The Special Touch College Preparatory model incorporates Financial Awareness through life-skill training, money, financial goals, investment, retirement, death and living benefits, and college funding. Special Touch believes that financial literacy at a young age decreases poverty and teaches students knowledge when it comes to being the best with their money as adults. Exposure to financial situations and how to control money allows children to become better servants over their finances as adults. This allows children to learn to save and make good investments with their money.

Exposure to financial situations and how to control money is an integral part of a student's life. The

CLLAIMM MODEL

CLLAIMM© program model offers a variety of tips, lessons, and techniques as well as hands on application within a real-world setting. Activities will be provided as well as real life examples and Biblical principles on money, stewardship, investing, and why it is important to begin to develop these skills now as a young person.

Early financial literacy is a strong point of the thrust of this part of the program. Starting early and finishing strong are key aspects to life-long habits and ideas around financial responsibility. Factors such as saving for the future, tithing, and techniques on how to save and invest money are taught. Exercising self-control and saving for retirement are some of the key points of the lessons.

Children who learn these skills early have the advantage of being able to apply these facets to all areas of their financial lives. Students will learn to be proactive in creating a healthy dialogue when it comes to money, such as how to save and make good investments through different financial strategies. Learning to build wealth is a major asset to one's family life. Students will learn to make their money powerful by learning at a young age to protect their families through life insurance and living benefits–not just for themselves, but for their families' future as well. It is said that the future is now: Within this aspect, the students will be trained how to identify good fiscal goals, how to develop financial goals, and how to invest money for short and long-term plans. College savings and retirement are also addressed, as it is fiscally wise to start to develop and implement these goals within a child's early years, thus giving ample time to plant good seeds and watch them grow over time.

Poverty is a very real problem in many communities. The CLLAIMM© program model endeavors to empower and inspire students to be proactive about eradicating poverty. There are many causes to poverty, and the solutions to poverty are not easy to address. However, starting early, with a good plan, students can be catapulted into financial success using the tools presented in the CLLAIMM © program model. Students' financial success throughout their lives will drive out poverty and the problems that often accompany it. Students' will become better stewards of money as adults, bringing them full-circle in the community. Learning to save and making good investments is part of that aim.

CLLAIMM© Recycling Initiative

Recycling is a vital component to sustaining our earth and our environment. Students, faculty, and staff are encouraged to recycle whenever an opportunity presents itself.

CLLAIMM MODEL

Students are exposed to the recycling process and the school is encouraged to use recycled products whenever available.

It is important for students to understand how recycling, reducing, and reusing materials helps the earth and future generations. Students learn how to reduce their carbon footprint and how to make sustainable choices as consumers who wish to impact the earth for the greater good.

Integrity with recycling is an aspect that the CLLAIMM© program model desires to address, and students and staff are encouraged to become knowledgeable in ways they can facilitate healthier choices for our communities around recycling, sustainability, and "greener" choices. Going green and green energy choices are the future to helping create sustainable energy in our world. Students and staff are encouraged to research and implement these practices.

3. Leadership Empowerment (Empowerment)

CLLAIMM© model is designed to develop and empower leaders. It is also designed to promote entrepreneurship while supporting the concept of owning a business.

The leadership program is designed to build high leadership achievers. This program will contribute to teaching and training as students are introduced to various positions in schools. The experience of the Student will play a major role when it comes to the running of the school. As staff assist the students teaching them skills that would allow the student to eventually work independently.

Teachers assign students various roles and responsibilities. This program empowers students to become leaders by taking on administrative duties and by learning how to use small office equipment, classroom equipment, and what it takes to create organizational ethics within any institution. These skills enhance students' knowledge and interest in planning to be business owners, as well to attend great colleges or trade schools while promoting innovative training for various positions.

Developing leaders is a key aspect to any leadership program. There is a difference between being a manager and being a leader. A major part of this goal is to develop well-rounded leaders who are highly respected, full of integrity, and continuously soaring to new heights. Providing hands on workshops, classes, lessons and readings about effective leadership as well as bringing in motivational leaders to speak to students about what leadership is and how to grow as a leader helping students develop, sharpen and enhance their God-given talents.

CLLAIMM MODEL

Empowering leaders after developing them is the next step in enhancing leaders. Leaders are empowered to take on small projects with guidance that will give them experience in successfully leading a team and large projects. Students are encouraged to take skills or leadership assessments that outline what their interests, and that identify what skills they have developed so that they may understand their own leadership capabilities as well as make good decisions choosing a position in a leadership field.

Promoting entrepreneurship is an important part of the CLLAIMM© program model. Entrepreneurship and the supporting of owning one's own business are important for financial freedom in the future. It helps to promote leadership and to hone in on a student's desires and dreams in life. Students will be given training in business models, how to open a small business, and key aspects to keep in mind when determining what type of business they may like to open. Other entrepreneurial information will also be studied, such as maintaining a positive cash flow, networking, branding, marketing, and sustainability in long-term business.

Leadership within the CLLAIMM© program model will also extend into classroom roles and school roles. Students will have the opportunity to rise to classroom and school leadership positions. Studies show that when students feel supported, heard, and encouraged within a school setting, their performance increases across the spectrum of learning. Students will be assigned and trained in various roles, depending on age level, ranging from classroom helpers, student government, class representatives, handling of lunch tickets, attendance running, clerical and office support, and media representation such as newsletters, websites, and portfolios. These leadership and administrative duties include how to use small and large office and classroom equipment help to create strong platforms that can be used later in resumes and in showcasing experience in leadership roles. This, in turn, will benefit students in long-term avenues as they take the skills learned through the CLLAIMM© program and use them in the community as volunteers in churches and in the workplace.

These skills, combined with the other skills being developed in this program, will help students learn what it takes to create organizational ethics within any institution. Accessibility, integrity, transparency, fiscal accountability, submitting to a supervisor, working on a team, timeliness in completing a goal, balancing small budgets, networking, and running teams and events are all leadership skills that help to contribute to promoting education through college, entrepreneurship, business owning, and great job performance.

4. Academics (Education)

In School Academics

CLLAIMM© program model offers a rigorous and enriching academic structure to support each student in achieving and exceeding education standards determined by the State of California, the Western Association of Schools and Colleges (WASC), and the Association of Christian School International.

CLLAIMM© program model prides itself on enriching the academic structure. The model seeks to empower students to reach their optimal success by offering a rich, cross curricular, academically rigorous program. Students are highly encouraged to use higher thinking in all lessons, activities, and discussions. State requirements are utilized as guidelines in all CLLAIMM© program model frameworks, and the model strives to exceed the state's standards, and the independent study standards. A rich, vibrant, and intellectually stimulating learning platform is a strong focus, and employing varying learning modalities and excellent, culturally relevant pedagogy empowers each student to soar to new heights by build confidence along the way.

Homework Program

CLLAIMM© has a research-based philosophy about homework. Studies show that homework is a meaningful part of the learning process through building a comprehensive model of church, school, and home. Homework creates a continuum of learning and seamless transition between school and home by building a partnership between educator, student, and parent. It is the aim of the CLLAIMM© program model to select projects that can bring the lessons learned at school off of the page and to life so that there will be a combination of academic assignments paired with enriching activities that brings meaning to what is learned in the classroom.

The world is our classroom, and there are fascinating applications to bringing the world of learning home. These activities and homework are age and developmentally appropriate, and provide a challenging and satisfying experience for the student. Homework is carefully selected and presented to students to supplement and support what is being learned in the classroom, and provides emphasis to grasp and hone concepts learned.

5. Innovative & Positive School Environment (Environment)

CLLAIMM© model for Innovation supports creativity and challenges students to think critically. Positive reinforcement for creativity and working to build a good learning environment encourages innovation and growth. The school environment supports leadership, responsibility, and entrepreneurship and diligently

CLLAIMM MODEL

works to consistently maintain an environment of high energy and learning.

Innovation supports creativity and challenges students to think critically. It enables students to think "outside of the box," to explore avenues of creativity that may be new, and to spark interest in other activities. Students using The CLLAIMM© model are supported in finding new, innovative, and creative ways to express themselves across the curriculum while honing critical thinking skills.

Studies have consistently shown that a school's environment has a great impact on student learning. Schools that succeed are infused with a good supportive environment where students feel confident in trying out new skills and exploring new projects. A school's physical appearance also has a wide influence upon students and fosters learning. Schools that have positive messages in the halls and classrooms, culturally relevant lessons, art, literature, and pedagogy truly inspire students to do their best. High expectations of teacher, staff, and school communities have an ideal impact upon students. Students should have a feeling of Godliness, safeness, and comfort when they come to school each day, which will help them to build and entrepreneurial spirit.

This positive environment supports leadership, responsibility, and entrepreneurship by allowing students to have chances to learn, grow, and express themselves and the skills that they are learning in a positive and encouraging environment. For many students this type to safety net is just what they need to feel safe to step out into the unknown. High levels of learning, and high expectations coupled with high creativity will create an environment where students are comfortable with who they are, and excited about learning. When students' affective filters are lowered and they are able to truly relax and be creative they will learn.

Meditation (Enrichment)

Student Meditation

At Special Touch College Preparatory we believe that meditation is a vital component to enriching the lives and learning experiences of our students, faculty, and staff. Our culture and society are so constantly bombarded with stimuli through television, radio, Internet, and other media outlets that are brains are constantly jumping so much that many of our children have been categorized as "stimulation junkies."

CLLAIMM© model adheres to a holistic, well-rounded education of the whole child. Meditation is a vital component to enriching lives and we firmly believe that taking time to center and quiet oneself is highly

CLLAIMM MODEL

important to the success of students. Meditation is a practice that helps to center and quiet a person—inside and out. It creates an opportunity for self-reflection, self-care, and inward retrospection. These are lifelong habits that can be extremely beneficial to people, regardless of age.

Children can benefit from meditation as it enables them to think deeply about where they are in life and to be centered and present. Meditation, as a learning experience, is helpful because it allows people to take time out daily for inward reflection and gleaning the truth in nature, in the environment, and in firmly rooted Biblical truths. Meditation helps to create peace and calm in people and to take time to reflect on what is going on around them. Students that are not "over stimulated" are able to glean more in the learning day and are able to have more positive outcomes in the classroom.

Meditation enriches group work and learning together by creating an environment of peace and calm in the classroom and in the school. It also allows students to be able to articulate what they are feeling, to be in touch with their feelings, and to be able to dialogue on common ground about some of the materials being presented.

CLLAIMM

Scriptures help when meditating because the CLLAIMM© model seeks to use Biblical truths, scripture, and character development based in the Word of God. The following are some examples of scriptural references to meditation as found in the Bible and are also examples of what will be utilized within the school environment:

The Bible says to meditate on the Word of God – Psalms 1:2 says "but delight is in the law of the Lord, and on His law he meditates day and night"

- *The Bible says to meditate on the works of God – Deuteronomy 32:4 says, "He is the Rock, his works are perfect, and all His ways are just.*
- *The Bible says to meditate on things that are pleasing to God – Psalms 19:14 says "May the words of my mouth and the meditation of my heart be pleasing in your sight, O Lord my Rock and my Redeemer"*

It is also helpful to include soft music, quiet chimes, or instrumental worship in order to usher in a time of peace, quiet, and tranquility while meditating on the Word of God. Other helpful tools are scriptural affirmations on the walls, quiet praise movement and dance, and other creative tools such as painting, art, and journaling while meditating on Scripture.

7. Motivational Speaking

CLLAIMM© supports an aggressive motivational speakers series. The goal is to encourage and inspire students of all ages to achieve at higher levels by breaking down key concepts of growth and life development. This process stems from Romans 10:17: "Faith comes by hearing…". Designing age appropriate and subject relative speaker events to constantly encourage and inspire students throughout the school year will keep students motivated and alert when it comes positive thinking.

Motivational Speaking is key to unlocking positive thinking in students. When children are exposed to a variety of positive and inspiring motivational speakers they will see first hand positive role models from whom they can glean lessons and tips for life. The CLLAIMM© program model will offer a variety of motivational speaking opportunities to students from a wide range of subjects and professions. Motivational speaking speaks to the whole person and crosses over a wide range of people. Motivational speaking also employs various learning styles such as visual, auditory, verbal, and kinesthetic modalities.

When students see others speaking they are encouraged to become better speakers because they can relate to mentors who are sharing their stories. This also encourages students not to be afraid to share their stories.

CLLAIMM

Public speaking has often been listed as the number one fear of many Americans. Exposure to motivational speaking can provide a platform for students to expand their horizons and to speak about themselves in a public forum as well as to their or other children as they grow.

Motivational Speaking also helps to encourage and inspire students of all ages to achieve more by breaking down key concepts of growth and life development. This process stems from Romans 10:17 "Faith comes by hearing." Students are able to hear encouraging messages and apply them to daily life across the spectrum of personal and academic life. Students will be able to highlight ways that they can share positively about themselves and in turn motivate other students as well to enhance the continuum of learning. Motivational speaking is used to inspire students throughout the school year.

CLLAIMM© believes in providing students a well-rounded education focusing on academics, but also life skill development for success.

CLLAIMM© model supports competitive athletics and sports program including football, basketball, baseball, volleyball, wrestling, softball, golf, cheerleading, swimming, and tennis.

CLLAIMM MODEL

Conclusion

CLLAIMM© model goal is to build winners by producing winners. I believe in order to produce great adults children need guidance that gives them structured exposure with well-balanced strategies. I believe the Christian foundation, Life skills, Leadership practice, Academics, Innovative and Positive School Environment, Meditation, and Motivational Speaking creates a well-balanced adult.

Biography of Marena Simmons Jones M.Ed.

CLLAIMM© MODEL was developed and founded by Marena Simmons in 2011 after 18 years in the early childhood and education industry.

Although Simmons had one natural birth, she housed and raised several children throughout the years who still call her mom today. In 1989 Simmons injured her back while at work and was faced with not knowing in which direction her life would was headed. Remembering to keep her faith, Simmons's strong belief and favorite words, "adversities lead us to our destiny," she kept in mind that God's purpose would unveil itself in another chapter of her life. Simmons returned to school and earned two degrees Criminal Justice–one in Law and one in Corrections.

BIOGRAPHY OF MARENA SIMMONS JONES M.ED.

Simmons learned that her struggles in school were not because she was doing something wrong during her earlier years in school, but that she had the learning disability Dyslexia. Knowing this fact changed Simmons's life, and she decided to help young children become their best. That same year she had a dream that would change many people's lives including her own.

It was in 1994 that Simmons had a dream of owning a Day Care School that she would one day expand into a large school. It was called Special Touch, and it was full of color, excitement, structure, early learning, confidence building, and early college preparation. Later, Simmons added music, sports, Christian character building, teamwork, and togetherness to enriched young children's lives.

Supporting her dream, Simmons pursued a career in Early Childhood Development and earned a certificate in the field. She became more interested in providing a structured learning environment for children, and found an overbearing love for wanting to provide a healthy learning environment for all children who would become a part of her life. It was at this point that she had a flash back of her first baby-sitting job at the age of eight. By the time she was fifteen she had been a babysitter for several families, even bringing home a friend's baby, which she watched for days at a time.

CLLAIMM

Special Touch would not just be for baby-sitting; it would be an early learning school preparing children in many ways for their future educational needs. Simmons vividly remembers waking from that dream and realized that she had found her purpose in life. After sharing her dream with her sister, she and her sister, using the encouraging foundation and entrepreneurship attitude from their mother, launched Special Touch Day Care #1 teaching Preschool through 3rd grade. Nine years later she founded Special Touch Home School #2, which also encompasses Preschool through 3rd grade. Together, the schools produced successful businesses, which have served the community for over 20 years.

Simmons has earned as Associate in Science in Criminal Justice- Law Enforcement and Corrections, a Certificate in Early Childhood Development, a Bachelor of Business Administration - Management, a Master of Education in Leadership Organizations, and is currently pursuing a Doctorate in Education.

www.ingramcontent.com/pod-product-compliance
Lightning Source LLC
Chambersburg PA
CBHW021215240426
43672CB00026B/329